MW00424079

At David C Cook, we equip the local church around
the corner and around the globe to make disciples.
Come see how we are working together—go to
**www.davidccook.com**. Thank you!

DAVID **C** COOK

*transforming lives together*

# SUDDENLY SiNGLE WORKBOOK

# SUDDENLY SiNGLE WORKBOOK

## BUILDING YOUR FUTURE AFTER DIVORCE

### KATHEY BATEY

DAVID C COOK
*transforming lives together*

SUDDENLY SINGLE WORKBOOK
Published by David C Cook
4050 Lee Vance Drive
Colorado Springs, CO 80918 U.S.A.

David C Cook U.K., Kingsway Communications
Eastbourne, East Sussex BN23 6NT, England

The graphic circle C logo is a registered trademark of David C Cook.

All rights reserved. Except for brief excerpts for review purposes,
no part of this book may be reproduced or used in any form
without written permission from the publisher.

Details in some stories have been changed to protect the identities of the persons involved.

Unless otherwise noted, Scripture quotations are taken from the Holy Bible, NEW
INTERNATIONAL VERSION®, NIV®. Copyright © 1973, 2011 by Biblica, Inc.® Used
by permission. All rights reserved worldwide. NEW INTERNATIONAL VERSION® and
NIV® are registered trademarks of Biblica, Inc. Use of either trademark for the offering of
goods or services requires the prior written consent of Biblica, Inc. Scripture quotations
marked ESV are taken from the ESV® Bible (The Holy Bible, English Standard Version®),
copyright © 2001 by Crossway, a publishing ministry of Good News Publishers. Used
by permission. All rights reserved; HCSB are taken from the Holman Christian Standard
Bible®, copyright © 1999, 2003 by Holman Bible Publishers. Used by permission. Holman
Christian Standard Bible®, Holman CSB®, and HCSB® are federally registered trademarks
of Holman Bible Publishers; KJV are taken from the King James Version of the Bible.
(Public Domain.); NASB are taken from the New American Standard Bible®, copyright
© 1960, 1995 by The Lockman Foundation. Used by permission. (www.Lockman.org);
NKJV are taken from the New King James Version®. Copyright © 1982 by Thomas Nelson.
Used by permission. All rights reserved; NLT are taken from the Holy Bible, New Living
Translation, copyright © 1996, 2007 by Tyndale House Foundation. Used by permission
of Tyndale House Publishers, Inc., Carol Stream, Illinois 60188. All rights reserved.

ISBN 978-1-4347-1174-8
eISBN 978-0-8307-7217-9

© 2018 Kathey Batey

The Team: Alice Crider, Margot Starbuck, Amy Konyndyk,
Diane Gardner, Rachael Stevenson, Susan Murdock
Cover Design: Nick Lee
Cover Photo: Getty Images

Printed in the United States of America
First Edition 2018

1 2 3 4 5 6 7 8 9 10

012818

*"For I know the plans I have for you" says the*
*LORD ... "to give you a future and a hope."*

Jeremiah 29:11 NLT

# CONTENTS

# WELCOME

Have you been trying to establish yourself and heal after your divorce? Are you ready to begin creating your future? Are you asking the question, "What now?"

*Suddenly Single Workbook: Building Your Future after Divorce* is an eight-week, self-guided program to help you to build a life you love. The workbook's purpose is to help you get your footing after divorce, gain a fresh vision, plan for your life ahead, and create a structure to get there.

As you have been going through the transition of divorce, you've spent a great deal of time managing the stresses of your life change, using your energy toward coping with a bad or difficult relationship, navigating the divorce process, or simply surviving. But this is a new day. This is your day. It's time to be proactive and intentional again instead of merely reacting to life. It's time to start building your new life.

This workbook is divided into eight weeklong sessions. Each week covers vital, life-changing topics that give you the tools and power to create your new life and discover yourself again!

Each week ends with an Authenticity Check where you can be honest with yourself, make key decisions, and determine the actions you are going to take. At week 7 you will set a date on the calendar to create your "New Life Declaration." This will be your goal and dream page that will establish and guide your future.

Options for using this workbook:

1. Work through the lessons alone at a weekly appointment you make with yourself.
2. Unpack the lessons with friends or a group, meeting weekly or biweekly to discuss them together. (Allow two hours and delegate a group facilitator.)

Below, fill in the day and time you will work on each unit. For the most effective sessions, find a peaceful place, create an undistracted time, and take this appointment seriously. If you are in a group, fill in the day your group will meet to discuss each unit:

Week 1: _____

Week 2: _____

Week 3: _____

Week 4: _____

Week 5: _____

Week 6: _____

Week 7: _____

Week 8: _____

Creating an intentional life takes vision, courage, and wisdom. It's not too late to discover God's will. Wherever you're going, God is already there, so all you need to do is follow Him. Allow your faith, dreams, skill set, and heart's yearning to help you discover all of your potential and the beautiful life God has planned for you.

# DECIDING TO BUILD YOUR NEW LIFE

As you build your new life, you must create a structure for your dreams, discipline, and determination to stand on. This involves a commitment to change what needs to be changed and to make the decisions that need to be made to gain control of your life. You have this unique opportunity to start all over again and create a life full of purpose and satisfaction—the way you were designed to live. And in the process, find your peace and joy.

> *You reveal the path of life to me; in Your presence is abundant joy; in your right hand are eternal pleasures.*
> Psalm 16:11 HCSB

## MY LIFE REDESIGNED

After a divorce, you wonder, *Where do I go from here? What now?* To answer that, you'll need to make an assertive, prayerful effort to create the life you want. Such an important journey requires total honesty of self, openness to direction, vulnerability, and responsibility. You must take control and commit your life to God, of you allow other people's expectations and agendas to determine your life. Be proactive, listen to *God's* direction, and do not be a reflex to the constant life stimuli coming at you. Use this workbook to dream, to decide, and to dwell in the space where God's will is for you. And choose to make the next chapter of your story the greatest one yet. It can be the best part of your life if you are willing to do the work and establish the structure to make it happen.

Let's begin by looking at your life and clarifying where you want to be. Add any thoughts, people, places, or things you want in your life:

I want to be aligned with:
- People who contribute good things to my life, such as: My friends, my mom, and sister
- Spiritual influences, such as: Pastor Lean, Meredith, Bethel church
- Intellectual stimulation, such as: prayer, study, reading, healing.
- People whose lives I can contribute to, such as: My children, my friends
- People who allow me space to be vulnerable, such as: my mom, Meredith, my psychologist
- Healthy boundaries for myself and others, such as: Limited Contact w/ Richard

I want to be defined by:

- Meeting the expectations and goals I have for myself, such as: _professionalism, real, respectful, joyful, upfront_
- The quality of my character, such as: _kind, accepting, joyful_
- The kindness and love I show a needy world by: _giving, empathetic, available, guiry_
- The contribution I make to better my world as I: _heal, rely on God, feel God in my life_

I was designed to:

- Creatively use my skills and gifts to contribute to the world in ways like: _mediate, be happy, worship, be joyful, playful_
- Be a masterpiece of my Creator who made me, shown by: _my art, my children_
- Fulfill my potential by: _exploring me, being me._
- Need others as I: _grow, heal, build a new life_
- Love others by: _sharing, loving, supporting_

16

# GIVE YOURSELF PERMISSION

Before you begin building your new life, you have to give yourself permission to be honest, direct, raw, vulnerable, and real. Remove all expectations your family and others have for you, and even some of the expectations you have for yourself. Don't come into this process with defenses up, being the brave soldier with a stiff upper lip. Put down your guns. Be curious about who you are now and what you want in your future.

Go easy on yourself—especially when emotions you have stuffed down for so long begin to surface. Don't be judgmental or harsh when you face uncomfortable and difficult issues. Let the issues, hurts, goals, and big dreams come up. Only this way can you gain power over your life by facing all of your "stuff." Permit yourself to simply be God's child and to explore and discover, in childlike faith, all you are and all your soul longs for. Ask God the tough questions. It will take courage, but you cannot step into a focused future without it. You may need to isolate yourself from some people in order to look honestly at your life so their influence doesn't direct you.

# ASSESSING YOUR FUTURE

The assessment you're about to do is for your eyes and use only. It is a tool to determine where you are now and how you want to build your future. But you must know where "here" is before you can reach the "there" God has in store. In this questionnaire, you are lovingly giving yourself permission to honestly open up your heart.

Week 1 will be the most extensive of the eight weeks. Give this assessment the time it needs. Don't rush through it, but ponder what your heart wants to say and what your soul needs. Give yourself at least a full undistracted hour to complete the assessment. This is your life; it's worth the time and effort to plan for it.

Some questions may seem simplistic but they are important. It may be the first time you've asked yourself such questions. If not, it will help to review your responses to them. Answer them honestly, without shame, blame, or guilt. If you are in a group, you may share what you feel relevant to share.

Are you ready? Take a deep breath, clear your head and heart, and let's begin.

# THE ASSESSMENT

## *Feelings*

*As he thinketh in his heart, so is he.*
Proverbs 23:7 KJV

How would you describe your life overall right now? (Examples: I'm relatively content but wanting more, unsettled, sad, angry, depressed, unsure what I want, undefined, directionless, without a strong feeling either way, etc.)

*I'm unsure of what I want. I want my feeling secure to limited and broken. I want to feel happy and whole. I want security.*

How are you doing right now in these areas?
- Physical health _so/so - need more excersize_
- Intellectual stimulation _good_
- Spiritual peace _growing, engaged_
- Emotional health _engaged, working through feelings_

Although each area is important, which of these areas are the most prominent to you right now?

_Spiritual and emotional health. I really want to heal. Fix what I've caused for a long time, fix what I've denied and run from._

Are you living your life in faith or in fear? Describe what that means to you.

_Much more in faith than ever before. I feel connected to God._

In what area of life do you feel successful right now?

_My profession. My family life feels broken. I feel inempt in fixing it. God I give you my family heal us, heal us all._

In what area of your life do you feel there is something lacking?

My family feely whole, healed, settled.
My sons fight, they don't help w/o push.
Jill misses Needledin
Mickey is agressive
Everything Feels Hard.

In the past six months, when were you the happiest?

With my children and friends / family -
Dawdling, being altogether. At church
feeling God's holy spirit.

What made this time or occasion happy? (Security, relationship, status, etc.)

Being w/ people who love us. Being
Together, having the ability to go
and do.

What is your biggest fear right now?

- Not being financially secure
- Not having my little kids
  3/4 of the time

How could this fear be calmed? Is there an external force that can calm your fear, or does it need to come from within?

God provides

Legal documents completed hopefully.

_____

_____

What do you hold on to when you are afraid?

God

friends / family

_____

_____

## Relationships

Have you created a support system in your life? If not, why not? If so, how?

Yes - friends and family

_____

_____

Who within your network of family and friends would you consider to be part of your true support system?

My mom and sister

_____

_____

Do you have a best friend—someone you confide in who allows you to be totally open, vulnerable, and unguarded? If so, who is that person and how honest do you allow yourself to be with him or her?

_Leta is great we have had very similar experiences. She is very understandely_

Are you as social as you want to be?

_Yes and No_
_I'd like to be more._

What social activities are you currently participating in?

_- chatting mainly_
_- occassionally going out_

What new social activities would you like to participate in?

_- Performances_
_- music_
_- dinner parties_
_- church activities_

In social settings, do you seek out people or do you wait for people to approach you?

_I wait for them. I need to build up and seek people out._

Do you have a significant other in your life? How does this person enhance your life? Or do they add stress to your life?

_No - my ex is a stress. I felt demurred and criticed regularly. I struggled to be comfortable._

How does this companion treat you? Is this acceptable to you?

_It wasn't acceptable. I left. Still I miss having a companion. I wish for a true friend, partner._

How does this companion encourage you?

_He did not. He didn't want me doing anything or speaking or going out_

Is there something missing that you would like to see happen in this relationship? If so, what?

_love, intimacy, trust, laughter,
activities together, friendship, copying
friends together_

## Finances

On a scale of one to ten, how would you rate your total debt? (one = bankrupt/unmanageable; five = balanced and controlled; ten = very little debt/debt free) _3 - high debt, single income._

What debt causes you the most concern right now?

_credit card debt. Not enough
money ea. month to cover expenses_

What do you see as your biggest financial issue to face going forward?

_paying off debt, student loan,
car payment, divorce_

Are you optimistic about your financial future? Explain.

Do-Do depending on how the divorce goes. if it's drawn out. it will be worse.

Do you consider yourself a spender, saver, hoarder, or well-balanced in spending?

Spender/saver - I like to do activities, have nice belongings, clothes. I also want to save and have money in the bank.

What is one specific financial goal you have for the upcoming year?

- pay off 1/2 my debt at least. 30000 this year. 30000 next.
- live w/i my budget.
- save money every year 12000.00

Are you an emotional purchaser? What does your emotional purchasing look like?

- Yes. Amazon kids items. Clothing
- food. liquor

What money-tracking system do you use for budgeting, and does it work for you?

_Ramsey's monthly budget app yes I like it._

What research have you done to find another money-tracking system that might work better for you?

_- I could tally all purchases to see where my money is going._

## Children

If you have children, list their names and one word to describe your relationship (such as _healthy, rescuing, distant, argumentative, loving, supportive, nurturing_, etc.).

_Jillian - loving          Step Children_
_Michael - nurturing       Christina - distant_
_Abram - supportive        Paul - distant_
_Mario - supportive + argumentative_

What are your most joyful times with your children?

_Going camping, going to the beach. Playing in the yard. Mantracker, hiking, bonfires. board games, card games, movie nights. Banff._

How often do you encourage them to talk about their goals and dreams?

*Regularly - I love hearing about their ideas, plans, goals.*

Do they know you have dreams for yourself as well as dreams for them?

*Probably not. They see me work hard.*

Have you ever shared your dreams and hopes for your future with your children?

*I'm not sure what they are. I'm stuck in the past. I'm grieving. My future - I want to become a therapist. I want friends and family active in my life and spending regular time together.*

What are your points of tension with your children?

*When they don't listen. If they refuse to participate in activities I'm trying to make family routines*

When do these points of tension occur?

Sometimes daily. Sometimes weekly. Sometimes monthly.

What could help to reduce this tension?

A little compliance, a little more help around the house.

Who is your support network in raising your children? Or are you parenting alone?

Parenting alone - Richard is available for the little kids somewhat. I haven't found a group for me & my ans, but I do have supportive friends

## Direction

What core values are the most important to you? (For example, honesty, kindness, independence, etc.) List them here.

Kindness, generosity, reciprocal love, forgiveness, love, self growth acceptance, honesty to self and others. being responsible

What is one goal you want to reach with the rest of your life?

_Joy. Living intimate relationship_
_Close relationships_

Do you have an expressed theme or a defined purpose in your life?
If so, what is it?

_Genuine warmth, consideration,_
_truth sayer, changemaker._
_Growth_

What unfinished business is holding you back from living the life
you want (finances, relationships, lack of forgiveness, fear, unbelief,
other people's expectations)?

_financial security. Self confidence,_
_forgiveness of self and others._

Have you ever developed a mission statement for your life? Can you
write it out? The mission of my life is to _Be connected to_
_God. Be a light, grow and give._
_Be Joyful, Feel Satisfaction._

If you want help writing a mission statement, answer the following questions.

What do I know as absolute truth for my life?

God is with me.
God is Good.

What makes me feel fulfilled and gives me purpose?

My children, number one purpose.
Helping others but it's changing. I
want it to be based on my gifts of
talents moreso then caretaker. I'm too
tired to caretake anymore.

To what and whom am I utterly committed?

My children, God, my sister, my mother

How do I define success?

Having people in my life who love
me, genuinely know me.
Doing the best job I can and feeling
good about it.

What important things do I want to accomplish in my life?

Becoming a CS supervisor.
Learning to paint, do pottery
Holidays annually w/ my family
Owning my home.
Having an active social network - genuine ppl

What three foundational spiritual truths do I believe in?

- God is grace
- We have a purpose - be a kind person.
- God will provide - away, a means, a direction.

What long-lasting dream am I striving for?

Joy and Happy heart. Satisfaction

What important relationships am I devoted to and spending time and energy on?

My relationship w/ God
My relationship w/ my children.
My relationship w/ Leah + Mom.

Whom will I serve?

_God - when asked_
_My children_

What are my guideposts, morals, and ethics in my life?

_Be open, be honest, speak your_
_truth. we all have something we_
_are struggly w/ be kind._

Now go back and write out a mission statement that fits your responses (see p. 29).

How would you take this mission statement and turn it into a vision for the next ten years?

## Control

Are you satisfied with the control you have in your life?

What is one thing you would change in your life to have more control?

_____

_____

_____

_____

How much control do you currently have to make this change?

_____

_____

_____

_____

Is there a power struggle in your life? With whom? Who's winning?

_____

_____

_____

_____

How have you dealt with your past life challenges? Have you ever thought you wanted to change how you deal with current challenges?

_____

_____

_____

_____

What challenge have you experienced you don't feel you handled well? What lessons did you take to heart to handle the issue differently in the future?

_____

_____

_____

_____

Can you state, "I have a clear vision and I know exactly the direction I want my life to go"? Why or why not?

_____

_____

_____

_____

Define what you want for the rest of your story and what you want your life story to be. Be bold!

_____

_____

_____

_____

As you look at your life right now, what is one thing for which you can say, "This is not what I want in my life"?

_____

_____

_____

_____

Do you have self-defeating or self-sabotaging behavior in your life? What is it, and do you know why you do it? Was this behavior taught or is it your own coping skill?

_____

_____

_____

_____

What healthy risks have you taken in the last year to help yourself grow?

_____

_____

_____

_____

Do you believe that risk is necessary for you to grow? Explain.

_____

_____

_____

_____

## REVIEW YOUR ASSESSMENT

How do you feel about your life after taking this assessment? (Circle where appropriate.)

Discontented/Hate my life                                    Love my life

1                    2                    3                    4                    5

What area of your life jumps out as positive?

_____

_____

_____

_____

What jumps out as negative?

_____

_____

_____

_____

What area(s) would you like to change?

_____

_____

_____

_____

How ready and committed are you to make changes in order to create your new life?

_____

_____

_____

_____

# WHAT IT TAKES TO BE READY

Until you are ready to change, nothing will change. What does it mean to be *ready*? This acronym explains.

### Risk

You must be willing to take risks because nothing changes without risk. When you are willing to take risks, you are ready to move forward and make changes in your life.

### Enough

When you realize you are *enough* and you have *enough* to create a great life, you are ready to move forward and make changes. Stop clawing to be more. You are enough in who you are.

### Action

You have to *do* something to make change. When you have made your plan of action, you then need to take action. You must *do* something to move forward before your life can change.

### Determination

When you are determined to focus and stop giving excuses for your life or letting others determine your life, you are ready to move forward and make changes in your life.

## *Yearning*

When you begin to listen to your heart's longing and trust your gut and your God, you are ready to move forward and make changes in your life. Stop being led by others and listen to your own soul.

# WEEK 1 AUTHENTICITY CHECK

This section, completed at the end of each week, will help you determine and develop a plan to achieve your life goals.

In light of the assessment and what I have considered this week, what are the:

Decisions I need to make?

_____

_____

_____

_____

Actions I need to take?

_____

_____

_____

_____

Things I can no longer tolerate?

_____

_____

_____

_____

Ideas and areas I should nurture and develop?

_____

_____

_____

_____

Things I am grateful for?

_____

_____

_____

_____

Thoughts I have on what these decisions will mean for my future?

_____

_____

_____

_____

# MY PRAYER STRATEGY FOR THIS WEEK

As you devise a prayer strategy, give God access to each area of your life by (1) setting a determined time; (2) deciding how you will pray

(Scripture study, meditation, praying a psalm, etc.); and (3) listing whom and what you will pray about.

When I'll pray:

_____

_____

_____

_____

How I'll pray:

_____

_____

_____

_____

What I'll pray about:

_____

_____

_____

_____

Lord, help me see what needs to be seen this week. When I bring my needs and requests into Your marvelous light, I can see them clearly and prioritized correctly. Thank You that You desire to give me wisdom and long for me to have a powerful life in Christ. Amen.

*The Lord is near. Do not be anxious about anything, but in every situation, by prayer and petition, with thanksgiving, present your requests to God. And the peace of God, which transcends all understanding, will guard your hearts and your minds in Christ Jesus.*

—Philippians 4:5–7

# MATTERS OF THE HEART

Julie had to move after her divorce. She couldn't afford the large house. As difficult as letting go of her past life was, she decided to take a positive approach. With each piece of furniture or item she added to the pile for the garage sale, she felt a relief in the purging. She was making way for new opportunities in her life. She was determined to make it simpler than it was in her past, so she could manage it more easily.

## SIMPLIFY TO CLARIFY

It's time to simplify your life in order to clarify what is important and worth your time and attention. If you want to build and change your life, you need to declutter it and get rid of the old to make space for the new.

Look at the things in your life that require upkeep, energy, and time and may be holding you back and bogging you down. What material things clutter the space around you and pull on you emotionally and/or physically? What things are packed away and unused that you haven't seen for years?

Some things don't fit in your life anymore, and it's time for them to go. Look at the physical objects you own and the space you inhabit. Is the extra, unused stuff benefiting you or distracting you?

Ask yourself:

- Do these things help me get where I want to go?
- Are they weighing me down because they're too heavy or require too much space, money, and time?
- Do they bring me enough joy or functionality to keep them?
- Could releasing them make space for a new focus in my future?

It takes honesty and courage to evaluate what's working and what's not. But the process is worth it. Notice what's not working, then let it go. Life is too short to hold on to that which is holding on to you!

## *My Physical Space*

As you consider your living space, do you have clutter *areas*? Office? Kitchen? Basement? Closet? Other? List such areas here.

_____

_____

_____

_____

Where is your special "clutter spot," the default place for everything?

_____

_____

_____

_____

What freedom of time and space would you enjoy if you purged the unnecessary clutter?

_____

_____

_____

_____

What freedom of time and space might you find if you focused more on the essentials of your life?

_____

_____

_____

_____

## *Clutter of the Heart*

The clutter of our living spaces often reflects the clutter of our lives and hearts. Heart clutter may be the messy struggles we are having, the lack of discipline in our thoughts, unresolved relationship issues, or the beliefs we hold about ourselves and our limitations. Many of these things, like the clutter in our home, need to be purged.

It's been forty years since Allan was abused. But you would have thought it was yesterday as he spoke in great detail of the injustice. He readily shared his hatred for his father. He thought his divorce confirmed what his father said—he wouldn't amount to much. If Allan was ever going to heal from his divorce, he had to remove some clutter about his past from his head. He had to stop believing his father's lies and uncover the truth of this divorce. It wasn't easy, but it was necessary for Allan to move forward. He needed counseling to understand the truth and to realize his father was wrong.

The best way to start clearing the clutter in your mind is by concentrating on God and His truth. God promises peace to those whose minds are focused according to His will:

> *You will keep in perfect peace those whose minds*
> *are steadfast, because they trust in you.*
> —Isaiah 26:3

As we home in on God's truth, He will help us sort through the "junk." The emotions or attitudes that clutter your heart are rarely obvious, and your human survival mode may have stuffed the heart clutter well, but they are still there. Start by asking yourself this: Which of the following emotions or attitudes clutter my heart right now? Which of them would I be brave enough to surrender?

- Blame: "It's my fault" or "It's their fault." Fault-finding is a trap you put yourself in.
- Anger: Fury against the injustice you cannot control or a past you cannot change.

- Jealousy: "Everyone else has it all together" or "She's got it all." Not seeing the power and beauty of your own blessings and strengths.
- Procrastination: "I'll do that tomorrow." Putting off getting help or doing what you know will help you heal and grow.
- Negative thoughts and talk: "I'm ugly, so stupid; I can never do things right." No self-compassion. These can be blatant or subtle.
- Shame: "I'm a disappointment; I don't live up to expectations; it's all my fault." Not giving yourself grace and love.
- Guilt: "I've failed; I've sinned too many times." Not seeing the power of the cross or that God's mercy is new every morning.
- Self-doubt: "God can't do anything important with my life." Forgetting you're His creation and His child and how much of a miracle you already are.
- Pessimism: "I'm stuck this way forever; there is nothing good in my life." Ignoring or denying God's promise for your future.
- Unforgiveness: "I will never let him or her forget this." Imprisoning yourself.
- Other: maybe God is showing you other emotions or attitudes that are not listed here.

List the specific things you need to let go of:

_____

_____

_____

_____

Are you willing to let go of these things, or will you cling to what is poisoning you and holding you back?

Emotional "junk" distracts us from what is important. It zaps our time, energy, and attention. Is this clutter distracting you from what really matters? How can you see the vision for your life when so much of your view is blocked? Would living uncluttered in your mental space—your thoughts, attitudes, and feelings—give you unhindered connection to God and make a powerful difference for you?

Your power is in decluttering your past not in harboring it within. Underneath all that clutter is a new life. Will you free yourself to find it?

Allan's life teaches the importance of forgiveness and decluttering the emotions and attitudes that will fester and harm you if they are not dealt with. Purge them out of your life. How? Only God can reach this deep space to heal it, but He will only do it with your permission. Tell God exactly what you're willing to release to Him. You don't have to know *how* you will do it, but trust He will guide and show you the way out. And then you have to take that faith and trust, and take a step out. As you trust, try praying this prayer: "Lord, today I submit to You the baggage that has slowed me down. Give me the power to give it to You, and rid this heart of these worthless distractions from the glorious things You have planned for me."

# FACING FEAR

Going through divorce creates anxiety and a fear of an unknown future. Our imaginations can run to the negative instead of searching for the positive. This is where we must be proactive. We can manage our fears by faith and trusting the Scriptures and start building a new life.

Our fears are often the reason we don't take risks, so let's understand what those fears are so we can stop them from strangling us. By facing our fears we can learn to control them. Comfort and care for yourself as you admit these fears. Pray for a new perspective and the strength to subdue your fears so they will help you rather than hinder you.

Understanding your fears is also a way to understand yourself better. Marilyn French says: "Fear is a question. What are you afraid of and why? Our fears are a treasure house of self-knowledge if we explore them."[1]

Consider where your fears come from. What might they be trying to teach you?

_____

_____

_____

_____

To calm your fears, claim your God-given power: "For God has not given us a spirit of fear, but of power and of love and of a sound mind" (2 Tim. 1:7 NKJV).

Some fears guard us from harm. Fear of doing wrong can be healthy. Fear of prison and hell is healthy. Fear of driving in the wrong lane on a blind hill could save your life. Determine which fears are healthy and guard you from trouble and which fears hold you back from a powerful life, such as fear of failing, fear of what other people think, fear of not being perfect, or fear of taking any risks that will lead you into a new life.

What are your fears in the areas below? Consider what God would want for you in these areas. And then, if you are willing, commit them to God:

Emotions: _____

Relationships: _____

Finances: _____

Children: _____

Career: _____

Spiritual Life: _____

Physical Health: _____

Intellectual Life: _____

Future: _____

It may not be sudden, but each step (even the little ones) move you forward to a new and better life. It takes courage to face fear. But you do not have to go alone. Pray and take your Savior with you.

# THE BAGGAGE OF UNFORGIVENESS

An unwillingness to forgive the person who hurt you will paralyze your ability to create your future. When you refuse to forgive, you remain stuck, emotionally and spiritually. Forgiveness frees *you*. But it does not let anyone out of their responsibility for the hurt they caused or condone what happened. But it releases you.

Unforgiveness does not give you power over the situation; it stops you from moving forward. You will be unable to absorb the present and discover your future to the fullest if you hold on to the clutter of unforgiveness. And who wants to miss out on what God has in store? It's simply not worth it. Do you have time to lose or give away to someone else who is taking up space in your head?

## *Forgiveness*
Is there someone you need to forgive? Who is it?

_____

_____

_____

_____

Does this person deserve forgiveness? Consider, none of us deserved Christ's forgiveness. But we received it. To what degree does considering Christ's forgiveness help you consider and forgive the person who doesn't deserve it?

_____

_____

_____

_____

What practical things can you do to help you forgive? Are there words to tell yourself or Scripture to claim, or could you confide in a pastor or friend?

_____

_____

_____

_____

Sometimes actually telling someone you forgive them isn't wise or safe. You may find yourself in a victim role all over again. Seek some guidance if you choose to forgive someone in person. Rehearse what you will say to them. You can forgive without the other person ever knowing, if it is necessary to keep you physically and emotionally safe.

Forgiveness depends totally upon you. Try praying the following: "Lord, only You understand the depth of pain I feel and carry. Lord, it is too heavy and too ugly for me to bear. I am asking Your Spirit to lift this burden from me once and for all. I know You are justice, and You know every detail of what happened. But Lord I ask for Your Spirit of forgiveness to take over and take away the pain I lug around all the time, and for Your Spirit to lift my head to the unrestrained future You have for me."

## *A Final Sweep*

You've come this far, and you have some points of tension that need to be resolved. Don't worry if it seems a bit overwhelming at times. Take a break if you need to. Don't rush this process. In fact, you may want to return to this workbook in three months or a year. But for this week, pause to take one more look. Is there anything else in your mental or emotional space that needs to go?

This season is your opportunity to build a life you love. This is your moment. Think about your beautiful new future, and describe what you want that future to include.

What I want to live in my heart:

_____

_____

_____

_____

What I choose to release from my heart:

_____

_____

_____

_____

# WEEK 2 AUTHENTICITY CHECK

In light of the clutter of my home and heart, I have determined the following this week:

The most important decisions I need to make:

_____

_____

_____

_____

The actions I need to take:

_____

_____

_____

_____

Things I can no longer tolerate:

_____

_____

_____

_____

Some ideas and areas I will nurture and develop:

_____

_____

_____

_____

Things I am grateful for:

_____

_____

_____

_____

One thought on what these decisions will mean for my future:

_____

_____

_____

_____

# MY PRAYER STRATEGY FOR THIS WEEK

When I'll pray:

_____

_____

_____

_____

How I'll pray:

_____

_____

_____

_____

What I'll pray about:

_____

_____

_____

_____

Lord, give me strength to recognize what to release so I can move forward into the life You have for me, unhindered. (Write out your own prayer of "good riddance.")

*Those who cleanse themselves ... will be instruments for special purposes, made holy, useful to the Master and prepared to do any good work. Flee the evil desires of youth and pursue righteousness, faith, love and peace, along with those who call on the Lord out of a pure heart.*

—2 Timothy 2:21–22

# MANAGING YOUR FINANCES

Jim found himself broke after the divorce. The only ones who won financially through this process were the lawyers. Where would he even begin when he'd lost the house, had no savings, and had a low-paying job? His young children were confused and disoriented. Jim knew the only way he would survive would be to master the skill of money management. He went to his church, and they sponsored him taking finance classes where he learned to use the envelope system. (With the envelope system, you designate an envelope for every expense and place the money you need in the designated envelope when you are paid each week or month.) Years later when I met up with Jim again, he had a new job, he'd rented a small apartment for his family, and his children had attended DC4K (Divorce Care for Kids). He was content and grateful for how far he and his children had come. He worked; God provided.

Finances are a major part of life and a major concern for all of us, especially as our lives change through divorce. How can you leverage this life change, play it smart, and stay strong (or at least survive) financially? Although it is not easy, it is doable.

# WHEN YOU CONTROL YOUR FINANCES, YOU CONTROL YOUR LIFE

As your life changes, your finances will too. There may be one income instead of two and two houses instead of one. If you can stay within your income, you will make it through this tumultuous time. However, if you spend beyond your means, especially now, you will compound your troubles and heartaches. Your attitude drives your budget, and emotional purchasing can devastate you financially. You may still be financially vulnerable right now, with unknown expenses and unknown factors from this life change. Proceed with caution.

Similar to any other fear, our financial fears can cause our instincts of fight, flight, or freeze to kick in. Flight is running away from the problem and avoiding the discipline of budgeting. Freeze is when we become paralyzed, do nothing, and hope things will change by themselves. Fight is the only way out. When we face finances head on and take control of them, we conquer them so they won't conquer us.

If you take charge of your budget and your spending, you can have more choices and not be a slave to debt. God knows the peace, strength, and freedom that financial prudence brings, and He wants that for you.

You can do this, regardless of the number of zeros in your budget! The less you have, the more creative you become. Life will become more calm and predictable soon, but especially now, start to live within your means.

Let your frustration and anger toward the circumstances move you to be disciplined and to conquer your debt. Find shortcuts, negotiate, shop for bargains, and discover consignment and resale shops around you. Be

- defiant against the world's marketing persuasion and social pressures.
- determined to control your finances to live powerfully.
- debt-free so you have control and choices.

Financially secure people have more choices and more freedom.

## WISDOM DURING TRANSITION

Be aware that times of transition or emotional upheaval often cause great financial vulnerability. If possible, make the major decisions after the dust of the divorce has settled. You will be thinking clearer and have found the equilibrium of your new life. One exception: make sure you separate your finances from your former spouse as quickly as possible. This is critical to establishing your new life.

Take a quick look at your income versus your "outgo." Use the chart below to map out your debt, expenses, and income.

| Debt: (payment for ongoing obligations) | Weekly | Monthly | Quarterly | Annually |
|---|---|---|---|---|
| Car | | | | |
| Rent/mortgage | | | | |
| Student loans | | | | |
| Credit Card(s) | | | | |
| Expenses: (Current spending) | | | | |
| Food, gas, clothing | | | | |
| Utilities, phone, cable, internet | | | | |
| Insurances (house, car, health, disability, etc.) | | | | |
| Entertainment and "fun fund" (lattes, movies, eating out) | | | | |
| Totals | | | | |

What is your monthly debt payment?      $_____

How much are your monthly expenses?      $_____

What is the total of debt and expenses?      $_____

How much is your monthly income?      $_____

Does the math work? _____

What debt will you focus on first?

_____
_____
_____
_____

Are there creative shortcuts for your essential debt?

_____
_____
_____
_____

Have you ever consulted with a financial guide? If not, what steps will you take to find solid financial advice? If you've seen a financial advisor, how might going back to them be beneficial now?

_____
_____
_____
_____

In what ways could you revise your debt to reduce it faster? (Pay extra? Sell? Share?)

_____
_____
_____
_____

What expenses can be monitored more closely and reduced to meet your budget or pay down debt?

_____

_____

_____

_____

# LIVING FREE

Ellen went on a cruise with a girlfriend, bought a new (to her) car, developed her own business, and gave to the needy in her community. And she paid cash for all of those things. How did she do that? Because for years, she carefully managed her money. Her goal was to live so if the worst scenario came, she could work at the local coffee shop to survive if she had to and live a life in her control. She crushed her debts. Her children lived modestly and joined the game of frugality with their mother.

How you handle your money matters because money controls how you can live. Ellen doesn't go on cruises every year; she went on this one because she got a great deal. She doesn't buy brand new cars or make millions in her business. But she is in control and has a peace that people with more money would envy. She trusts God and gives Him the credit and the tithe.

How do you trust God with your finances?

_____

_____

_____

_____

Describe your vision of what debt-free living would look like for you, and describe how powerful you would feel. What would you do with the extra time, money, and choices?

_____

_____

_____

_____

## *Pay Attention to How You Spend*

What is your attitude toward finances and controlling your spending? The following questions will help you recognize any pitfalls or habits that can keep you from taking charge of your finances.

*Credit Cards*
- Are you using them for survival?
- Are you using them for convenience?
- Are you using them for tracking or bookkeeping?
- Do you have the best credit card for low interest and cash back?
- Are you using them wisely?

*Cash*

- Do you pay fees to retrieve cash regularly from an ATM? How often?
- How do you keep track of your cash spending?
- Are you using it wisely?

*Checks*

- Do you still write checks? Do you keep complete records in your check register?
- Do you pay extra late fees on bills or bounce checks?
- Are you using checks wisely?

*Online Payment Methods*

- Do you make online purchases for convenience?
- Do you overspend online because it is a "too easy" spending method for you? Or do you have it under control?
- Are you using online payments wisely?

*Other*

- What other spending areas trip you up?

# INSURANCE

Hannah looked for ways to cut costs. She debated cutting health or car insurance. Fortunately, she paid both using payment plans the providers helped her find by increasing the deductible and making monthly payments. And she kept them current. Later that year, she had a car accident that put her son in the hospital. She is certain now that insurances are not areas to cut.

Thankfully Hannah's son only had a short stay in the hospital. If it had been longer and she had been without insurance, Hannah may have found herself in a very deep financial hole that would take decades to dig out of.

## *Evaluate Your Insurance Coverage*

Who is your insurance carrier? Do you trust your insurance provider? Do you understand your insurance coverage (medical, auto, home, life)? If you don't, make an appointment with your insurance provider to get your questions answered.

Are you over-insured or under-insured? If you don't know, make a note to contact your insurance provider and find out.

_____

_____

_____

_____

Have you compared your insurance policy with different companies for the best benefit and price for you? If not, plan to do it soon. Because insurance companies compete with each other, you may find better coverage for less with a new company. This is true for medical, home, auto, and life insurances.

# EMERGENCY SAVINGS

Emergencies happen. It's only a question of when and if you can handle it financially. But you can plan ahead to be prepared for an emergency. An emergency fund should be your top priority after paying your monthly bills.

How much money do you need to live on for one month? Include your house payment, car payment, groceries, electricity, insurances, clothing, and kids' lunches—every item.

Now figure this amount for three months. (Ideally six months would be better, if you can, but a minimum of three months.) This is your emergency account goal that needs to be readily accessible in the event of an emergency (for example, job loss, illness, car problems, flooded basement, etc.).

Medical expenses are the number one reason for personal bankruptcy.[2] Do you have the necessary funds for a medical emergency?

Base your medical emergency funds by the coverage of your health insurance plan. Understand the deductibles and copays and their implications. For example, if you have a Health Savings Account (HSA) you have a high deductible, which could result in a lot of unplanned expenses if the annual timing is off. (If you are sick in December and then again in January, you could be required to meet your full deductible twice in a short period of time.) If you are off work for a length of time this too could result in unplanned expenses.

What is your goal for having sufficient savings for medical emergencies?

_____

_____

_____

_____

If you don't yet have a sufficient emergency savings fund, what is your goal amount and how might you begin to save more over time?

_____

_____

_____

# FUTURE PLANNING

Think of a woman you know whose husband takes care of all the finances. What happens to her when she is on her own through divorce? Was this you? How will you seek help?

Gather information on these accounts:

|  | Location of Funds | Current Value | Gains (Interest, investments, etc.) | Management of Funds (How are they paid? Contact information.) |
|---|---|---|---|---|
| **401K** |  |  |  |  |
| **Roth IRA** |  |  |  |  |
| **Checking, Savings, CDs, Special Bank Accounts** |  |  |  |  |
| **HSA** |  |  |  |  |
| **College fund for kids** |  |  |  |  |
| **Will** |  |  |  |  |
| **Trust** |  |  |  |  |
| **Other** |  |  |  |  |

Here is a list of definitions for these terms in simple form:

- 401K, 403b—employer-sponsored retirement funds
- Roth IRA—investments deposited after tax so they are withdrawn tax free
- Traditional IRA—invested pre-tax, grows tax free; payout is taxed
- Checking, savings, CDs, special bank accounts— short-term investments easily accessible to you

- HSA—Health Savings Accounts accompany a high-deductible plan used for medical emergencies (tax free)
- College fund for kids—529 (for education only) or Roth IRA, which has tax-saving benefits

If this section leads to more questions than answers, you should seek a financial counselor. Inquire of your church, trusted friends, or reliable coworker as to whom they would recommend (ask for a teacher, not a salesperson).

Do you have an updated will, letter of last instruction, or patient advocate forms (such as a durable medical power of attorney or advanced directive)? If not, they will need to be done. This is a vulnerable area for many single people. Take your former spouse off your will, confirm the beneficiaries, and check to see if you want to change the executor of your will. These forms are available online and may not require a lawyer to create them for you. Give age-appropriate direction to your children.

# FINANCIAL GOALS

Setting financial goals for yourself will allow you to work toward financial freedom, which means more choices for you instead of being enslaved to debt. Envisioning a goal will help keep you on track and sustain you when life's unexpected expenses come up. And financially, you can always expect the unexpected.

What are your specific financial goals? (For example, get out of debt, start a college fund for the kids, buy a house, purchase a new car.)

_____

_____

_____

_____

Which of these financial goals would you like to achieve …
Over the next year?

_____

_____

_____

_____

Over the next five years?

_____

_____

_____

_____

Over the next ten years?

_____

_____

_____

_____

# FINANCIAL NETWORK

During and after divorce, you need support in every area of your life, and you'd be wise to create a financial network if you don't already have one. The following questions will help you determine what you already have in place and what or whom you may need to seek out.

Who is in your financial network (advisors, banks, credit unions, investors, family, etc.)?

_____

_____

_____

_____

Who is your closest confidant in money matters?

_____

_____

_____

_____

Who in your life makes good money decisions?

_____

_____

_____

_____

What wise financial decisions did they make that intrigue you and earned your respect?

_____

_____

_____

_____

Whom do you turn to first when you have a financial question or concern, and why?

_____

_____

_____

_____

Who will tell you the financial truth you may not want to hear?

_____

_____

_____

_____

What system do you use to track your budget, investments, and other financial concerns?

_____

_____

_____

_____

Is it working? _____

If not, find a new money-managing system and see what you can learn about better management. A good system should show you where your spending weaknesses are. There are many free systems online. Try a different system from the one you are currently using and see if it works better for you or if you learn something new in money management. There are many resources available, including books and classes. You don't have to do this alone.

# GOD CARES

God cares for you in every area of your life, including finances. You want control over your money, and God wants you to have control. Pray faithfully about your finances. Money is one of the most talked about subjects in the Scriptures. God does provide, but you are the steward to manage that provision and to honor Him through your decisions and actions. Pray for wisdom and provision.

# WEEK 3 AUTHENTICITY CHECK

In light of the financial management issues I considered this week, what are the:

Decisions I need to make?

_____

_____

_____

_____

Actions I need to take?

_____

_____

_____

_____

Things I can no longer tolerate?

_____

_____

_____

_____

Ideas and areas I should nurture and develop?

_____

_____

_____

_____

Things I'm grateful for?

_____

_____

_____

_____

Thoughts I have on what these decisions will mean for my future?

_____

_____

_____

_____

# MY PRAYER STRATEGY FOR THIS WEEK

When I'll pray:

_____

_____

_____

_____

How I'll pray:

_____

_____

_____

_____

What I'll pray about:

_____

_____

_____

_____

Lord, You say that where my treasure is, there my heart is also. Right now, I need guidance to help me see what treasure I have and to learn to depend on You to help manage it. Give my heart wisdom, Lord. Help me find my eternal treasure in You. Help me to gain strength, freedom, and wisdom in finances so I can stand strong, be unhindered, and be used by You.

*The kingdom of heaven is like treasure hidden in a field.*
*When a man found it, he hid it again, and then in his*
*joy went and sold all he had and bought that field.*
—Matthew 13:44

# DEVELOPING YOUR NEW SELF

Sam shared with the group his insecurities after the divorce. He admitted, "I feel like I'm an insecure teenager again, not knowing who I am or where I need to go. I hope this stage passes."

It does.

This is a painful time, but it is also a powerful one. It is a time of rawness that can make you moldable and teachable in a new and mysterious way. To make this dynamic time count, you have to be open to your new world and your new normal.

It's a *big* world out there. Realizing you live in a very small part of it, how will you broaden your circles to expand and open your life to new possibilities? How will you expose yourself and your mind to all the world has to offer you and all you have to offer your world?

Let's start exploring, defining, and designing!

# SPEAKING YOUR NEW LIFE INTO EXISTENCE

The words you speak to yourself and to others are powerful and have great influence.

What words have you been using to describe your past?

_____

_____

_____

_____

What positive words and statements are you speaking when you talk about your life plans and your future?

_____

_____

_____

_____

Which words empower you in a positive way?

_____

_____

_____

_____

Take some time to write out your dreams, goals, and plans.

_____

_____

_____

_____

You may be amazed at the connections you can make when you start speaking about your goals and intentions for the future instead of discussing your past. Talk about where you are going, not where you have been. You may find many people who want to help and support you. Talk about your goals, dreams, and life mission out loud.

# PERSONAL HEALTH HABITS

Stressful times can make you more vulnerable to illness. During such seasons it may be tempting to neglect yourself or use artificial means of relief that do not help you to promote a new life. How are you taking care of yourself right now? Are you doing anything in excess? One way to be compassionate toward yourself is to take care of your body.

Describe your current level of self-care in:

Nutrition:

_____

_____

_____

_____

Exercise:

_____

_____

_____

_____

Rest:

_____

_____

_____

_____

Stress Reduction:

_____

_____

_____

_____

Substance Avoidance:

_____

_____

_____

_____

Which area do you feel strongest in right now?

_____

_____

_____

Which area do you want to improve?

_____

_____

_____

In what way could you start now? Make one plan for this week and post it where you can see it every day of the week.

_____

_____

_____

## YOUR NETWORK

Your personal network is important because it will influence, lead, and expose you either to good things and positive decisions or negative things and wrong decisions. This is a great time to review your network, the people you allow into your life, and this is the best time to grow and expand your world!

Who is in your personal network? List the five people who are closest to you. (Quality matters more than quantity.)

_____

_____

_____

_____

Are they healthy people in their lifestyles, beliefs, and actions? Are they (or would they be) a positive influcence on your children?

_____

_____

_____

_____

Who or what do you spend time with to get advice, attitudes, and influence? (For example, TV, radio, Internet, social media, etc.)

_____

_____

_____

_____

What groups are you affiliated with and what cultures do you belong to? What influence do they have on you?

_____

_____

_____

_____

Would you be brave enough to venture out into the world to build a new network? Perhaps you've been intrigued by a few groups and have considered joining. What groups would these be?

_____

_____

_____

_____

Some groups you'd love to check out include:

_____

_____

_____

_____

Which of these are free and which have a cost? Would the cost be a good investment?

_____

_____

_____

_____

What is the commitment of time and money you will want or need to give?

_____

_____

_____

_____

What activities do you do alone and what do you do with others? Are you satisfied with the differential?

_____

_____

_____

_____

What fears do you have as you consider trying something new?

_____

_____

_____

_____

Fredrick Buechner wrote, "The place God calls you to is the place where your deep gladness and the world's deep hunger meet."[3] Where do you recognize this convergence in your life?

Why is reviewing and growing your network important now? Because you are forming and designing your new life, and you are seeking positive change and influence to build that life. The journey is meant to be one of joy.

The Scriptures tell us, "A joyful heart is good medicine, but a broken spirit dries up the bones" (Prov. 17:22 HCSB). As you design your new life, how can you give yourself permission to laugh more and not take life seriously all the time? Give yourself a minute to consider how you will make room for joy.

How do you—and how will you—find your joy? Are there new and creative ways to search it out?

_____

_____

_____

_____

*Take my yoke upon you and learn from me, for I am gentle and humble in heart, and you will find rest for your souls. For my yoke is easy and my burden is light.*
—Matthew 11:29–30

# SOCIAL OPPORTUNITIES

Nurturing your social life is important. Here you will create a new life and new relationships. Put yourself out there to begin developing bonds with people. Take on some leadership roles that allow you to grow. Don't wait to be asked; you can be the one to make the plans and ask. Invite people into your life. Initiate coffee with a friend, or host a dinner party. It doesn't have to be extravagant; it just has to be warm and inviting.

When you do put yourself out there with people, disappointing times will happen. (In fact, plan on it, so you won't be so surprised when it occurs.) But the lessons will go with you as you venture on and away from people who are not healthy for you or don't build you up.

What kind of new activity would you enjoy? Will you put it on your calendar this week?

_____

_____

_____

_____

Do you prefer spectating events, group discussion, one-on-one meetings, in-depth conversation, or something else?

_____

_____

_____

_____

# CONVERSATION SKILLS

Conversation is an art and, like other arts, many people do it but few of us do it really well. The art of conversation requires deeper discussion than "How is the weather?" or "How are you?" It requires honoring the other person, creating a safe place for people to be authentic and vulnerable if they choose to be, and sincere interest in other people's lives. It means being able to "volley" back attention to the person you are speaking with when they serve gracious comments and inquiries to you.

I'm convinced good conversation skills allow you to minister to people in very spiritual ways and should never be underestimated. As Dr. Henry Cloud said, "God created all of us to be change agents for each other. We have a responsibility to influence the people in our lives to be the best possible people they can be."[4]

Sometimes we say more when we say nothing at all. People are attracted to those who will listen to them. It makes your conversations unforgettable to other people. For the most meaningful discussions:

- Show interest in the other person's life—what they are passionate about, why they are passionate about it, their goals, their interests, and how they plan to get there. Don't leave statements hanging. If someone shares something from the heart, prompt further discussion with, "Tell me more," "Explain what you mean," or "I'd love to hear more about that."
- Make eye contact. Pay attention to the other person at a comfortable contact level for them.
- Be undistracted. We've all been part of a conversation that a cell phone or text interrupts. Giving in to phone calls or taking away attention tells the person they are second in importance.
- Limit the "I" in your conversation. Have you ever noticed how many times you say "I" when you speak to others? Is it so often that others surrender conversation and shut down?
- Take interest in others. Create good questions to engage someone in conversation.

- Listen empathetically. Listen with an understanding heart and try to see from their perspective what they are dealing with.

## How Conscientious Are You in Conversations?

Think about a conversation you had last week ...

With whom did you talk? Where?

_____

_____

_____

_____

How frequently did you say "I"?

_____

_____

_____

_____

How well did you listen for the pulse of their heart and spirit (how they are really doing)?

_____

_____

_____

_____

Did you discuss important issues or the ordinary and mundane?

_____

_____

_____

_____

Were you listening for periods of time, or did you do all the talking?

_____

_____

_____

_____

How did you honor, give attention to, or allow the other person to share his or her heart?

_____

_____

_____

_____

What kind of questions did you ask?

_____

_____

_____

_____

What did you share about yourself?

_____

_____

_____

_____

## *Interactive Listening Exercise*

This project allows you to talk about yourself beyond your roles (such as your profession, parent, or child) and to help you reconnect with who you are and talk about your strengths, goals, and dreams. It is also an exercise in deliberate listening skills.

If you are in a group, find a partner and give a five-minute talk about yourself. If you are doing this program alone, ask a friend to listen to you and explain the exercise.

The listener only asks questions for clarification and deeper detail. Each person gets an opportunity to speak and then to listen and ask questions for five minutes.

What to talk about:
- What are your talents? What do you do well?
- What do you like about yourself?
- What positive things do others say about you?
- How have you handled past challenges (aside from the divorce)?
- What was your proudest moment (involving you, not your children)?
- Where do you want to be one year from today?
- How would you describe your leadership abilities?

- What are your gifts and why do you believe they are your gifts?
- What did you want to be in college or high school? Have you done this or anything like it?

What not to talk about:
- Your divorce
- Your roles (profession, parent, child, sibling, etc.)
- Your ex-spouse

After five minutes of just listening, the listener asks questions for clarification and deeper detail.

Both participants should practice reflective listening (restating what the speaker has said). Paraphrase the speaker's words back to them by starting with, "What I hear you saying is …" or "Do I hear you saying …?" Use the person's name a couple of times. Keep direct eye contact where comfortable.

After the exercise, jot down a few notes about what you experienced or learned.

_____

_____

_____

_____

# GOD HAS GOOD PLANS FOR YOU

*God has given each of you a gift from his great variety of spiritual gifts. Use them well to serve one another.*
—1 Peter 4:10 NLT

God has a plan for you, and the sooner you search it out and cooperate with this glorious plan, the sooner you will be at peace and find fulfillment. His plan exceeds your highest dreams. His plan will strengthen you and contribute to others' lives.

What do you think God wants for you?

_____

_____

_____

_____

Have you ever thought it possible that God wants more for you than you do? Explain.

_____

_____

_____

_____

What have you learned about your relationship with God?

_____

_____

_____

_____

# WEEK 4 AUTHENTICITY CHECK

In light of what I considered this week, what are the:

Decisions I need to make?

_____
_____
_____
_____

Actions I need to take?

_____
_____
_____
_____

Things I can no longer tolerate?

_____
_____
_____
_____

What will these decisions mean for my future?

_____

_____

_____

_____

Ideas and areas I should nurture and develop?

_____

_____

_____

_____

Things I'm grateful for?

_____

_____

_____

_____

# MY PRAYER STRATEGY FOR THIS WEEK

When I'll pray:

_____

_____

_____

_____

How I'll pray:

_____

_____

_____

_____

What I'll pray about:

_____

_____

_____

_____

Lord God, You know my heart and what brings me joy and peace. In this big world there are people who can add to my life and there are lives that I can contribute to. Would You show me who they are and allow our paths to cross? Help me be in the places where good things come, and take me away from places that would distract or bring me harm. God, give me wisdom in relationships. Let me see the hearts that are good for me and the hearts I need to distance myself from; let me see the hearts I need to help and bless. Thank You that You want a powerful life for me. You want me to be more like Your Son who is the most pleasing to You. In this, I will find a successful, powerful servant's life.

*Blessed is the man who walks not in the counsel of the wicked, nor stands in the way of sinners, nor sits in the seat of scoffers; but his delight is in the law of the LORD, and on his law he meditates day and night.*

—Psalm 1:1–2 ESV

*Week 5*

# CREATING BOUNDARIES AND TAKING RISKS

If any two things in your life will change you and catapult you in the direction you want to go, it is the two areas you will work on this week—setting boundaries and taking risks. They may sound opposite, but they are two vital parts of life you can control. Both boundaries and risks guard and monitor what comes in and goes out of your heart, life, and influence.

I see divorced people harming themselves by not setting healthy boundaries with their ex-spouse, children, family, friends, and others. People take advantage of them or require their time and they end up emotionally and financially broken and hopeless.

It will take the Holy Spirit's wisdom and counsel to find hope and to see the need to set boundaries and the wisdom to take calculated risks. First, let's define boundaries and risk taking.

- Boundaries: Knowing what you are in control of and responsible for. This includes your feelings, life, decisions, choices, and the consequences of those choices. You only control your own stuff.

- Risk Taking: Seeing the potential and adventure in areas you can control and accepting your responsibility to create your own life. This includes trying new things even when you don't know the results, believing in your ability to do something different, experimenting with your life in smart and daring ways, and being vulnerable and authentic.

Guard your heart. Setting boundaries and taking risks give us control of our lives and create new opportunities. They guard, direct, and help us know when to open up and when to be cautious. We are to diligently guard what comes in and what goes out of our lives: "Above all else, guard your heart, for everything you do flows from it" (Prov. 4:23).

## PERSONAL BOUNDARIES THAT PROMOTE SELF-CARE

Having personal boundaries is one way we take care of ourselves. In case you have not practiced healthy boundaries in your past, give yourself permission to guard your heart and set boundaries to take care of yourself. You can say no. It may be difficult for you, but it may be the freedom your soul longs for. Allow others to deal with their own responsibilities and issues and to face the consequences of their own actions (including your children when age appropriate). You don't have to save the world. Jesus did that. Carry the burdens of those who need your help, but let those who need to carry their own weight, carry it. Many things can distract us, take us off course, waste our time, and distract us from our purpose. By setting boundaries we manage this—boundaries regarding what people ask or demand of us and to what extent we allow people to influence us.

Consider the boundaries you have or have not established as you answer the following questions:

Who do you allow into the personal areas of your life (finances, emotions, dreams)?

_____

_____

_____

_____

Whose presence and access do you limit in your life because they are not healthy?

_____

_____

_____

_____

Are there people you should separate from your life or give limited access to you? Are they unsafe for you? (Unsafe means more than just physically dangerous; they can be unsafe emotionally, spiritually, and professionally. It includes behavior that influences you negatively.)

_____

_____

_____

_____

What do you do to take care of your body? What unhealthy things do you limit?

_____

_____

_____

_____

What financial boundaries do you give yourself?

_____

_____

_____

_____

How do you take care of your soul? What do you guard against? What uplifts you?

_____

_____

_____

_____

Search the book of Proverbs and find a Bible verse you can claim to guide you to have healthy boundaries. Write it here.

_____

_____

_____

_____

# BOUNDARIES WITH PEOPLE

Joe is one of the most gregarious people I know. Everyone loves him. Joe builds trust; he helps me carry boxes into the church and pays attention to those who lead and those in need. But Joe is not safe. He earns people's trust and then asks them for money, rides, and the chance to stay a night at their place. God wants us to love the "Joes" of the world, but Joe can work—he has skills; he just prefers not to use them. He would rather be everyone's friend and allow others to meet his needs. As much as I'd like to help Joe, he must accept his own responsibility and handle his own life. I have to say, "No, Joe, I won't give you money or a ride across town. But I can help you look for a job."

We must love people. Some people, however, we must love from a distance. And some must be loved with strong boundaries.

Are there people in your life you are constantly rescuing? Who are they?

_____

_____

_____

_____

Are there people who regularly rescue you? How does this hinder you from growing?

_____

_____

_____

_____

To build your life anew you must set boundaries of respect for yourself and for others. It is a discipline of time, mind, and will. Without boundaries, you will lose all three.

What is one example of a situation when someone asked you to do something you didn't want to do or didn't have the time or resources to do?

_____

_____

_____

_____

How did you respond? Do you feel you handled it well?

_____

_____

_____

_____

How do you typically respond when people ask you to do things you don't want to do or you don't have time or the resources to do?

_____

_____

_____

_____

Another way to set boundaries in your life is to review your reactions to the actions of others. What is one example of a situation when someone treated you poorly? How did you respond?

_____

_____

_____

_____

What thoughts about yourself came to mind?

_____

_____

_____

_____

Who do you rescue so they don't have to face the consequences of their actions?

_____

_____

_____

_____

How will this harm them in the long run?

_____

_____

_____

_____

Has this person developed a dependence on you?

_____

_____

_____

_____

What specific things do you do for others they could do for themselves?

_____

_____

_____

_____

What would happen if you suddenly said no to doing something for someone they should do for themselves? Would it alter your relationship with them? In the long run, could it be more healthy and helpful for them?

_____

_____

_____

_____

Who are the people in your life you need to put into healthy perspective and possibly "love from a distance"?

_____

_____

_____

_____

How will you establish those boundaries today?

_____

_____

_____

_____

What boundaries in your relationships do you feel good about?

_____

_____

_____

_____

Who in your life can you ask to hold you accountable in promoting healthier boundaries?

_____

_____

_____

_____

Boundaries are there to help you focus your life not to exclude or disregard people. They also refine to whom you should minister and help you focus wholeheartedly in one direction instead of halfheartedly in multiple.

# MAINTAIN EXISTING HEALTHY RELATIONSHIPS

We need relationships. God created us for community. It is up to us to find those relationships that are life-giving or that we can give life to. Cherish the neighbor who watches your house while you're out of town and your same-sex friends who allow you to confide in them and who you can trust with your vulnerability.

What healthy relationships do you have now that are important to you to maintain?

_____

_____

_____

_____

# DEVELOPING HEALTHY NEW RELATIONSHIPS

Remember, boundaries aren't about keeping people out. Rather, they're about keeping you in a safe, healthy space so you can develop satisfying mutual relationships. There are so many options to spend your life on. You need to seek the Holy Spirit to show you what is most worthwhile for you.

In the space below, you will see your lifeline. Note your birth, childhood, young adulthood, marriage, and then your divorce. See the extended line after your divorce as the rest of the story of your life. It is open, full of potential, and full of adventures yet to come. There is still time to create the life you want, a life that is rich with purpose and joy.

*Childhood*        *Married life*        *Divorce*                    *The rest of my story*

Look at the open space you now have in which to write your story. The clearer you can define where you want your life to go, the better the chances are you will get there. Say yes to something better than being a reflex to your own life. Find your life in service to others by discovering your ministry and your focus. Then you will uncover your glorious purpose in your own story, which fits into God's story.

Who are some people you respect and would like to get to know?

_____

_____

_____

_____

How will you initiate and pursue relationship with them?

_____

_____

_____

_____

Find associations or groups that resonate with your heart or your talents and skills. Try attending a couple meetings before you decide if it's rght for you. Find those who inspire you or places you can join in their mission to make the world a better place. Who might that be?

_____

_____

_____

_____

# RISK TAKING

Nothing changes without risk. It is important not only to determine what you want but also to evaluate the risk that goes with it. If you don't do something different, nothing in your life will change. But wow, will it change when you take smart risks! Now is the time to decide what risk you need to take and the way God would have you go.

There is a risk with everything you want. Identify what you want and the risks you need to take to build your new life.

| What I Want ... | What I Have to Risk ... |
|---|---|
|  |  |
|  |  |
|  |  |
|  |  |
|  |  |
|  |  |
|  |  |

# WEEK 5 AUTHENTICITY CHECK

In light of what I considered this week, what are the:

Decisions I need to make?

_____

_____

_____

_____

Actions I need to take?

_____

_____

_____

Things I can no longer tolerate?

_____

_____

_____

_____

Ideas and areas I should nurture and develop?

_____

_____

_____

_____

Things I'm grateful for?

_____

_____

_____

My thoughts on what these decisions will mean for my future?

_____

_____

_____

# MY PRAYER STRATEGY FOR THIS WEEK

When I'll pray:

_____

_____

_____

_____

How I'll pray:

_____

_____

_____

_____

What I'll pray about:

_____

_____

_____

_____

Lord God, it takes wisdom to know where to set boundaries and when to take risks. I pray specifically for the relationships I am in—my children, my friends, and my community connections. Which do you see that I need to revise? Lord, teach me to always love. But some relationships take too much time and effort and distract me from what I am called to do for You. I need Your wisdom to help me see them. I want to be brave for You. You did not call us to be fearful or complacent. You called us to serve You through serving people. Show me my ministry, give me a glimpse of my new life, and give me a vision of the risks I need to take. Help me know when to be still and when to move forward and take risks.

*Wisdom cries aloud in the street, in the markets she raises her voice; at the head of the noisy streets she cries out; at the entrance of the city gates she speaks: "How long, O simple ones, will you love being simple? How long will scoffers delight in their scoffing and fools hate knowledge? If you turn at my reproof, behold, I will pour out my spirit to you; I will make my words known to you."*

—Proverbs 1:20–23 ESV

*Week 6*

# AVOIDING SELF-SABOTAGE, AFFIRMING SELF-WORTH

Do you ever wonder about God's thoughts toward you and your life transition?

God knows you intimately. He knows the number of hairs on your head and collects your tears (Matt. 10:30; Ps. 56:8; see also Ps. 139). He also knows the personal blessing and path He wants in your life. What does God have for you? God desires to give your life purpose. He desires that you have peace, wisdom, love, and an abundant life. His abundance may not be monetary riches; His abundance may be ministry, influence, relationships, peace, and a deep relationship with Him.

So how do you receive all of this and become all you are meant to be? By allowing Him access to every part of your life and taking Him at His word. "Be strong and courageous. Do not be afraid or terrified because of them, for the LORD your God goes with you; he will never leave you nor forsake you" (Deut. 31:6).

What does God want for you for the rest of your life? Through the Scriptures, this much we know:

- He wants you to accept His love for you. "Today, if you hear his voice, do not harden your hearts as you did in the rebellion" (Heb. 3:15). "The Father himself loves you because you have loved me and have believed that I came from God" (John 16:27).
- He wants you to have an intimate relationship with Him through His Son, Jesus Christ, for a life of purpose and direction that is full and eternal. "The thief comes only to steal and kill and destroy. I came that they may have life and have it abundantly" (John 10:10 ESV).
- He has an exciting plan for you. "For I know the plans I have for you, declares the LORD, plans for welfare and not for evil, to give you a future and a hope" (Jer. 29:11 ESV).
- He sends His Holy Spirit to be your closest companion to guide you and give you direction and truth. "And I will ask the Father, and he will give you another advocate to help you and be with you forever—the Spirit of truth.… But the Advocate, the Holy Spirit, whom the Father will send in my name, will teach you all things and will remind you of everything I have said to you" (John 14:16–17, 26).

- His Word (the Bible) is alive and will change your life when you receive it, just as it has changed the history of the world. "For the word of God is living and active, sharper than any two-edged sword, piercing to the division of soul and of spirit, of joints and of marrow, and discerning the thoughts and intentions of the heart" (Heb. 4:12 ESV).

# MARRIAGE AND SINGLENESS

What is your attitude toward singleness? Do you love it? Hate it? Are you tolerating it or celebrating it? What if there are more riches, experiences, and benefits for you in being single than being married? Would you be open to that?

Read 1 Corinthians 7:25–40.

In one sentence, describe what these verses mean to you.

_____

_____

_____

_____

What did Paul mean when he said it was better to stay on your own?

_____

_____

_____

_____

What did Paul mean when he said "undivided devotion to the Lord" (v. 35)?

_____

_____

_____

_____

How could this benefit you?

_____

_____

_____

_____

Today, what do you imagine God wants for you for the rest of your life?

_____

_____

_____

_____

What is your reaction to and belief about these thoughts from Paul?

_____

_____

_____

_____

How would your life be different if you truly trusted God with it?

_____

_____

_____

_____

# WHAT ABOUT YOUR SELF-SABOTAGING?

Sometimes the greatest enemy—who gets in the way, slows us down, trips us up, and lacks faith in us—is us. There are numerous ways we self-sabotage.

- Self-talk: we remind ourselves of our ineptness instead of our abilities.
- Not taking risks: we avoid opportunities that could change our life by giving in to fear.
- Believing lies about ourselves: we accept what someone else said about us, or what we think they think about us, as true, or believe part of a lie that is not entirely true.
- Looking for excuses: we don't chase after our greatness, saying we don't have time, money, intelligence, skill, or talent to make it happen.
- Fearing success: we don't know how we would handle success so we don't try. Or when we

succeed we downplay it, ruin it, or run away from it.

- Fearing being found out: we fear someone will find out we're ordinary and not that talented. We overlook our virtues and emphasize our weaknesses.

- Missing structure: we avoid the logistics needed to sharpen our skills.

- Avoiding discipline or boundaries: we don't commit the necessary time or space to grow our skills. We skim over the details.

- Procrastinating: we put things off until the last minute and then rush to finish. We excuse ourselves that it could have been better if we had more time. No wonder we deliver a mediocre product or not the best of us.

- Neglecting ourselves: we ignore our own needs, healthy eating, self-care, and sleep and then don't have the energy to perform at the optimal level.

As you look at these various self-sabotaging behaviors, which three do you recognize in your own life?

_____

_____

_____

_____

For each of the three methods you chose, answer these questions:

What benefits do you derive from this behavior? (There is always a payoff—comfort, excuses, or lessened fear, for example.)

_____

_____

_____

_____

What is your behavior costing you? (This could be your health, opportunities, relationships, emotional well-being, discovery and fulfillment of your potential, and more.)

_____

_____

_____

_____

Are you satisfied, or would you like to change the behavior? How will you start this week?

_____

_____

_____

_____

What change in your thoughts would you need to make in order to change the behavior? How will you prompt yourself when these thoughts appear?

_____

_____

_____

_____

Describe what would be different if you changed this behavior.

_____

_____

_____

Complete the chart on the next page for one of the three self-sabotaging behaviors you identified. Start with the circle in the center. Fill in this center circle with one way you sabotage yourself. In the extending circles, write how this behavior affects you in different areas (such as in your finances, work, health, etc.). Then move out to the next circle and chart how that behavior further branches out and affects your life. For example, you might write "Procrastinate on creating a budget" in the center circle. In the next circle out you might write "Spend too much on fancy coffee." And then in the next two circles, you might write "Can't take my daughter to a movie" and "Had to buy groceries on the credit card."

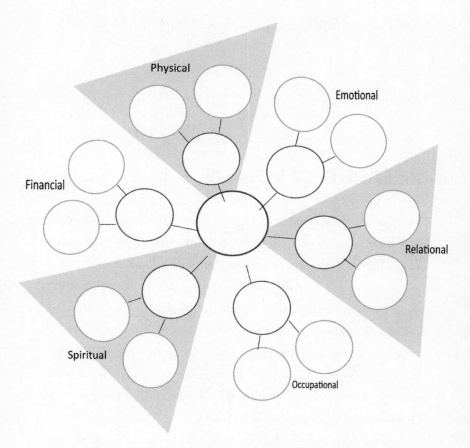

1. Think of an issue or concern you would like to change about yourself and write it in the center circle.
2. Note that this chart is divided up into the following six life areas: physical, emotional, relational, occupational, spiritual, and financial.
3. In the first level, write one consequence of the issue or concern in the middle for each of the six life areas.

4. Then look at what you wrote in the circles, and in the subsequent circles, write two consequences that result from what you wrote in the circles.
5. Stop and look at this map and note any insights you have regarding how the issue or concern in the center circle is impacting the other six areas of your life.

Adapted by Beth Bolthouse, LPC from various sources.

What area(s) affected or surprised you the most as you completed the circle chart?

_____

_____

_____

_____

# DEFEATING SABOTAGE

One reason I stress self-compassion is so we can drop our defenses, learn more about ourselves and our weaknesses, and then gently change them. If we can understand why we self-sabotage, we can replace sabotaging behavior with healthy behavior. Maybe it is our insecurity or the voices we've heard throughout life, or because we simply don't believe we deserve to have good things in life. God wants you to succeed. He wants good things in your life. He has compassion for you. Give yourself a break, embrace your own soul, and move forward into His grace. I bet you say things in your self-talk you would never say to anyone else.

Growth takes guts. To believe in yourself, your value, and all your wonderful potential requires courage. Celebrate your bravery when you try something new, whether you succeed or it doesn't work out.

Be gracious to yourself if you fail. Remember, no one leaves this world having lived perfectly. Stay close to God and you will succeed and remain on the right track. He holds blessings beyond your imagination in His right hand.

In what area would you rather fail than regret never having tried?

_____

_____

_____

_____

What three things can you say to yourself when you feel fearful or when sabotaging behaviors well up inside?

_____

_____

_____

_____

# HOW GOD SEES YOU

*Therefore, there is now no condemnation*
*for those who are in Christ Jesus.*
—Romans 8:1

Are you "in" Christ Jesus? Have you accepted Him into your life and asked Him to take all of your failures and sins and be your own personal Savior? There is where the power is for your life and where it always will be. You have freedom! Romans 8:1 (above) means you are under God's favor and not condemnation (judgment). *No condemnation.* So you contradict God's truth when you put judgment back on yourself! It is impossible for us to understand the final and eternal ramifications of this verse. We feel justified to beat ourselves up, to minimize our vision for our lives, and to limit what God desires for us.

Can you write a sentence stating that you face no condemnation? Use your name in the statement. Make it bold and beautiful.

_____

_____

_____

_____

Your condemnation, which you may stubbornly cling to in unbelief, is gone forever upon the cross of Christ. Trust this truth as your truth. Trust Him. He is trustworthy, I promise you.

> *See what great love the Father has lavished on*
> *us, that we should be called children of God!*
> *And this is what we are! The reason the world*
> *does not know us is that it did not know him.*
> —1 John 3:1

> *For God has not given us a spirit of fear, but*
> *of power and of love and of a sound mind.*
> —2 Timothy 1:7 NKJV

Which Scriptures mean the most to you as you claim the way God sees you? If you need help review the Psalms (especially Ps. 139).

_____

_____

_____

_____

Explain how you believe God sees you.

_____

_____

_____

_____

Do you sabotage yourself so you miss out on God's best for you?

_____

_____

_____

_____

How will you stop sabotaging yourself and see the potential God gave you?

_____

_____

_____

_____

How will you start acting on and living up to the potential God has placed in you?

_____

_____

_____

_____

Do you tell yourself God could not accept you as you are or do mighty things through you? Do you look in the mirror and dismiss yourself, thinking you'll be okay just to get by? Or do you celebrate yourself as God's special child?

_____

_____

_____

_____

Trust Him. Precious friend, there are only two places for your failures and sins—either on the cross or held within. You cannot handle it; Jesus can and did. If you need to stop here and accept that forgiveness for your life, please do. God's grace is too important to overlook as you're building your new life. It is where we find the freedom and the power to create our new, abundant, purposeful lives.

# WEEK 6 AUTHENTICITY CHECK

In light of what I considered this week, what are the:

Decisions I need to make?

_____

_____

_____

_____

Actions I need to take?

_____

_____

_____

_____

Things I can no longer tolerate?

_____

_____

_____

_____

Ideas and areas I should nurture and develop?

_____

_____

_____

_____

Things I'm grateful for?

_____

_____

_____

_____

My thoughts on what these decisions will mean for my future?

_____

_____

_____

_____

# MY PRAYER STRATEGY FOR THIS WEEK

When I'll pray:

_____

_____

_____

_____

How I'll pray:

_____

_____

_____

_____

What I'll pray about:

_____

_____

_____

_____

Lord God, You are *El Roi*, the God who sees me. Thank You that I cannot hide from You. You know my inward thoughts, my heart's desires, and how I stumble through Your blessings. Give me assurance that You accept me through the righteousness of Christ. So I may have the freedom to live a powerful life, give me the vision of acceptance and a vision of my life in You so I can begin to build my life upon You. Amen.

*You will keep in perfect peace those whose minds are steadfast,*
*because they trust in you. Trust in the LORD forever, for*
*the LORD, the LORD himself, is the Rock eternal.*
—Isaiah 26:3–4

*Week 7*

# BUILDING NEW HERITAGE HABITS

Have you noticed the older you get the more you recognize traits in yourself like those in your mom or dad? Those idiosyncrasies you swore you would never repeat, that are now naturally in your lifestyle and routines? The words, actions, habits, attitudes—they all show up without your permission!

We carry with us traits and beliefs we unconsciously learned by example. It is important to examine them to see if they should be perpetuated or extinguished. Many of these are spiritual struggles that require God's power to recognize, cease, and replace with something new.

Your heritage habits, even those you swore you'd never repeat, will continue without your consent until you look into them deliberately and conscientiously. It's okay to live out your heritage habits and hang-ups if you do it consciously and by your decision rather than by default.

# MY HERITAGE HABITS

What are the obvious behaviors you inherited from your family? (These can be personal attributes like having a sharp tongue or self-consciousness, perfectionism or attitudes toward food, work, death, etc.)

_____

_____

_____

_____

As you try to discern some of your heritage habits, it can help to look at your family's core values. The goal is to understand where you came from and how that still influences you today. What were your family's core values? What was the most important to them?

_____

_____

_____

_____

What behaviors, people, or accomplishments were celebrated when you were a child?

_____

_____

_____

_____

What behavior were you disciplined for when you were a child?

_____

_____

_____

_____

What was mocked when you were a child?

_____

_____

_____

_____

What was talked about when other people were discussed? (Successes, failures, rebellion, dress, actions, etc.)

_____

_____

_____

_____

Was there affection shown in your family? How (words, touch, etc.)?

_____

_____

_____

_____

How was money management taught?

_____
_____
_____
_____

Which emotions were allowed (tears, fears, struggles)? Or were emotions squelched and not allowed?

_____
_____
_____
_____

How was anger displayed in your home?

_____
_____
_____
_____

Was yelling or physical violence acceptable in disagreements?

_____
_____
_____
_____

Which adults helped you recognize and express your feelings? How?

_____

_____

_____

_____

Did adults discourage you from noticing and expressing your feelings? How?

_____

_____

_____

_____

Children absorb the emotional climate in their homes. Looking back today, with adult eyes, think about yourself as a child.

Describe the climate of your childhood home in one, two, or three words (loving, rigid, silly, angry, scary, safe, etc.).

_____          _____          _____

How were the topics listed below viewed in your household? Were they open for discussion, closed, not taught, strictly taught, very important, not honored, or something else? In the blanks below, write a word or two that describes how each issue was viewed in your family. How do you view them now?

Values
- Family:
  Then _____
  Now _____
- Roles of men:
  Then _____
  Now _____
- Roles of women:
  Then _____
  Now _____
- Roles of children:
  Then _____
  Now _____
- Work ethic:
  Then _____
  Now _____
- Honesty:
  Then _____
  Now _____
- Integrity:
  Then _____
  Now _____
- Kindness:
  Then _____
  Now _____
- Loyalty:
  Then _____
  Now _____

- Friendship:
  Then _____
  Now _____
- Other cultures:
  Then _____
  Now _____
- Other (list any others you identify):
  Then _____
  Now _____

Beliefs
- Money:
- Sex:
- Education:
- Safety:
- Showing affection:
- Religion:
- Emotions:
- Following rules:
- Obeying laws:
- Prejudices:
- Nutrition:

Behaviors
- Addiction:
- Emotional abuse:
- Physical abuse:
- Sexual abuse:

- Lying:
- Cursing:
- Yelling:
- Door slamming:
- Work ethic:
- Respect:
- Other:

Write down a memory or anecdote from your childhood that reflects one of the heritage traits you identified.

_____

_____

_____

_____

In what ways do you see the heritage habits (traditions, attitudes, beliefs, etc.) that are positive and life-giving reflected in your own household today?

_____

_____

_____

_____

In what ways do you see the heritage habits (traditions, attitudes, beliefs, etc) that are not positive, reflected in your household today?

_____

_____

_____

_____

Return to chapter 6 and look at the circles you drew to indicate self-sabotage. Are any of these heritage habits? This is not to blame or shame anyone, but simply to help you detach from those attitudes and attributes that need to cease.

Describe how your heritage impacted your self-sabotaging habits:

_____

_____

_____

_____

# DOING IT DIFFERENTLY

God created us to model after our parents, and then our children after us. It works beautifully when we have perfect parents. However, none of us had perfect parents, and we aren't perfect parents either. So something has to be done to stop the heritage habits that are not God honoring or beneficial to anyone. In fact, they hurt us. For the most part, we are blind to them. It will take the Holy Spirit and your determination to rid your life and your children's lives of the negative influences you had and may be recreating with your children now.

But you can end unhealthy practices and change your heritage and legacy. It can be done and done well through the power of the Holy Spirit.

Those who were never hugged can learn to hug. Those who were not shown how to deal with anger can learn to resolve problems without violence. The attitudes we were taught can change when we recognize them and we adopt better ways. Your legacy does not have a hold on you; you have a hold on it, and you can let it go.

We search to understand our heritage not to blame our parents or shame ourselves. Chances are, your parents did the best they could with the knowledge and resources they had. I know mine did, and I know my former husband and I did. Yet it is our responsibility to deal with what we have been given and to determine where we have to heal and what traits we have to deal with and not perpetuate. You are unbound from heritage habits when you are in Christ. Claim this truth, and ask God to show you what needs to be redeemed from your past and what you need to adapt and change to move forward to your future. I assure you it will take awareness and a willingness to do this. But the freedom and future blessing it brings is well worth it.

God redeems completely. In Christ, we are a new creation. That means we are born again, without the marks of the past. No one is born with scars. We are not born again with them either.

What heritage habits from your family of origin have you intentionally changed in your family as an adult? For example: let's say alcoholism was a central influence and power in your family. You decide not to allow alcohol to be a part of your heritage, so you ban all alcohol in your home and around your children. This would be changing your legacy by stopping the heritage. Another example may be honesty about money, and you decide to be upfront and truthful about all your income.

_____

_____

_____

_____

## GOD REMEMBERS YOUR CHILDHOOD TOO

God knows your childhood—the joys, pains, and injustices you experienced. If you comprehend your long-held misbeliefs and recognize the inner dialogue that echoes from your past, you can totally change the trajectory of your life journey. Only God is able to make something beautiful from these experiences. However, it takes a consciousness of what is there that needs to be dealt with and a willingness to surrender so you can rid it from yourself, your heritage to your children, and your world.

The best news is God wants you to end the influence of this hurtful past. As Christ said, "The truth will set you free" (John 8:32). That truth is you belong to Him with a perfect heritage. So discover how you think, search for the misbeliefs, and hear the inner dialogue so you can change the messages and alter the behaviors. Some people carry some heavy loads in their heritage. But God doesn't want us to carry it. As Joyce Meyer said in her book *Beauty for Ashes*, "God wants you to be delivered from what you have done and from what has been done to you—both are equally important to Him."[5]

Are there parts of yourself that must be surrendered to a new heritage or a stronger, more definitive heritage?

_____

_____

_____

_____

To help you change those unhealthy patterns, look again at the network of people you associate with. Do they help you become stronger than your heritage, or do they keep you bound to an old life?

_____

_____

_____

_____

*And God is able to bless you abundantly, so that in all things at all times, having all that you need, you will abound in every good work.*
—2 Corinthians 9:8

# WEEK 7 AUTHENTICITY CHECK

In light of what I considered this week of the power of my heritage habits, what are the:

Decisions I need to make?

_____

_____

_____

_____

Actions I need to take?

_____

_____

_____

_____

Things I can no longer tolerate?

_____

_____

_____

_____

Ideas and areas I should nurture and develop?

_____

_____

Things I am grateful for?

_____

_____

_____

_____

My thoughts on what these decisions will mean for my future?

_____

_____

_____

_____

# MY PRAYER STRATEGY FOR THIS WEEK

When I'll pray:

_____

_____

_____

How I'll pray:

_____

_____

_____

_____

What I'll pray about:

_____

_____

_____

_____

God, intervene in my heritage and my life! Open my eyes to see what is worthless, what is vain, and what is precious and good and needs to continue through the generations. Make my heritage great, make it influential, and make it glorifying to You. For in You alone will I find peace, purpose, and position.

*Therefore, if anyone is in Christ, he is a new creation.*
*The old has passed away; behold, the new has come.*
—2 Corinthians 5:17 ESV

*Week 8*

# COMPOSING YOUR NEW LIFE DECLARATION

Over the past seven weeks, you have worked on many important issues in your life and recorded them on your Authenticity Checks. Did a theme arise from these pages regarding the changes, decisions, and actions you need to make? Now is the time to cement these decisions into a strong declaration of what your new life will be. Claim it boldly. Honor this declaration like you honor and keep your promises to everyone else. And commit to it.

Life gets sucked up with duties, work, overcommitment, other people's plans, life demands, and laundry! This will be your own personal constitution to refer back to when or if you wander away from who you are. At the end you must face yourself and how you spent your life, and ultimately, you will face God to give an account. This declaration will give you the structure and focus you need. As these weeks conclude, I pray you will find the peace and direction God would have for you.

# PREPARING TO WRITE YOUR NEW LIFE DECLARATION

As you prepare to write your New Life Declaration, schedule a day on your calendar to work on it. Be intentional. Go away from your usual surroundings; find a quiet place where you can be undistracted—the water's edge, a quaint downtown area, a park with a picnic table. Go somewhere you love and where you can really focus, and consider what you wish to declare. Plan on a minimum of three hours. This is too important to rush.

As you begin your declaration, review the Authenticity Checks you completed. What did your heart speak? What decisions do you need to make and what actions do you need to take? What do you want for the rest of your story? What does God want you to do? What does He want for you? If you won't take this step now, when will you?

There is no perfect time for changes, but now can be your perfect time to claim your new life before more years pass by. Look at each Authenticity Check, mark them with sticky notes or, if necessary, tear them out of the workbook so you can review all of them together.

When you are in your special place, begin by reading the following. (Men, for you the visitor in the story is a man.)

An old woman appears in the doorway, white hair, shoulders bent, fragile hands. She looks oddly familiar, and you think, *Do I know her from somewhere and I just can't remember?* As she approaches, you get this sense that you do know her. She lifts her hand to take your hands and squeezes them firmly. You feel a surprising instant connection.

She leads you to sit on the couch beside her, all the while watching the steps she takes. She lifts her head, leans forward, and looks directly into your eyes. Suddenly the hair on the back of your neck stands up. By some strange supernatural phenomenon, you are staring at yourself at the end of your life. You have indeed grown old; with soft wrinkles around your eyes and mouth. You see for the first time your mortality.

She holds your hand. "What do you want me to feel at this point?" she asks. "What truly mattered? What should I be the most proud of? What are you doing now to bring peace for yourself for when you get here, at this time in your life? Whom did I truly touch with my life? Whom did I love with all my heart? Who carries my message from here? How does my life stand with God here and now?"

Write your thoughts and answers to her questions:

_____

_____

_____

_____

You make promises and commitments to everyone else. This time, make a promise and commitment to yourself. Make it in faith that God will honor it as you honor Him.

## YOUR INVITATION

In this quiet, undistracted moment, you are invited to enjoy rest, peace, and love. You may not know you're invited, but deep inside you may long to accept. It is the authentic and ultimate invitation, and it asks for your response.

## Accept the Ultimate Love for You

*For God so loved the world that He gave His only begotten Son, that whoever believes in Him should not perish but have everlasting life.*

—John 3:16 NKJV

## Accept the Ultimate Provision for You

*But God demonstrates His own love toward us, in that while we were yet sinners, Christ died for us. Much more then, having now been justified by His blood, we shall be saved from the wrath of God through Him.*

—Romans 5:8–9 NASB

*If you declare with your mouth, "Jesus is Lord," and believe in your heart that God raised him from the dead, you will be saved. For it is with your heart that you believe and are justified, and it is with your mouth that you profess your faith and are saved.*

—Romans 10:9–10

## Accept the Ultimate Purpose for You

*And we know that God causes all things to work together for good to those who love God, to those who are called according to His purpose.*

—Romans 8:28 NASB

*But you, dear friends, by building yourselves up in your most holy faith and praying in the Holy Spirit, keep yourselves in God's love as you wait for the mercy of our Lord Jesus Christ to bring you to eternal life.*
—Jude 20–21

# MY LIFE DECLARATION

This is my life declaration and the commitment I made to myself:

*This is my New Life Declaration. The past has passed. I leave behind all that needs to cease. I grasp all that is to come. I am embracing my future by committing to the following actions to create my new life. And through the power of Jesus Christ, I will do this.*

*I will replace my self-talk with Scripture. I claim 2 Timothy 1:7 as my life verse. I will post it, speak it, and trust it to guide me.*

*I will create distance from [name a specific person] to protect my spirit. I will love her "from a distance" because she is unsafe to me emotionally.*

*I will get out of debt beginning with my Visa credit card. I will pay triple the minimum and stop using this card for unnecessary shopping. I will make myself accountable to my friend John because he knows my finances and is trustworthy.*

*I will begin studying how I can start my new business by ...*

## NOW IT'S YOUR TURN

In this declaration I proclaim my *new life*. My story *starts now*; the past has only led me here to this powerful moment.

In alignment with my Authenticity Checks, my commitment to building my new life, and my desire to live powerfully, these are the decisions I have made:

_____

_____

_____

_____

These decisions I still must make to live a powerful life of purpose:

_____

_____

_____

_____

These actions I will take to live a powerful life of purpose:

_____

_____

_____

_____

Here is how I will begin now:

_____

_____

_____

_____

This week I will:

_____

_____

_____

_____

Next month, to keep me on track and accountable, I will:

_____

_____

_____

_____

What these decisions will mean for my future is:

_____

_____

_____

_____

To honor these commitments, I have spoken them before God, and I will share them with (my sibling, pastor, best friend, support group, or whoever I am comfortable with):

_____

_____

_____

_____

In relation to these commitments, I will take these actions starting on this date:

_____

_____

_____

_____

As I commit myself in this declaration, I thank God who wants great things for me as well as an intimate relationship with me. To the extent I am able and with the faith I have, I will allow God's input and control over my life. I ask for faith to allow Him to meet me where I am now and teach me to trust Him more. I commit my trust in Him as my God who knows the way I will go and has prepared many blessings as I follow Him.

Note: When sharing in a group, the group should lovingly ask questions to clarify any statement that is vague or nondescriptive.

# GO LIVE YOUR NEW LIFE!

Copy this declaration and post it somewhere you can see it. Refer to it often and hold up your weekly activities to see if it matches what you have declared. If it does, you are on the right track to your new life. If it does not, it's time to review the weekly Authenticity Checks to see where you wandered from the decisions and actions you determined.

I pray these past eight weeks have allowed you to honestly review where you are and determine what you want your life to be in Christ. You do not go out alone. The Holy Spirit will guide you if you allow Him to. Remember the decisions you have made. They are sacred to you, and if you committed them to Him, they are sacred to God. Live your life powerfully by having the discipline and the structure to empower it and to impact your world. God bless you as you journey and take on your world; it needs all that you have to give.

# NOTES

1. Marilyn French, "Fear Is a Question Quotes," searchquotes.com, accessed August 17, 2017, www.searchquotes.com/search/Fear_Is_A_Question/.

2. Mark P. Cussen, "Top Five Reasons People Go Bankrupt," *Investopedia*, March 19, 2010, www.investopedia.com/financial-edge/0310/top-5-reasons-people -go-bankrupt.aspx?ad=dirN&qo=investopediaSiteSearch&qsrc=0&o=40186.

3. Frederick Buechner, *Wishful Thinking: A Seeker's ABC* (San Francisco: HarperOne, 1993), 398.

4. Henry Cloud, *How to Have That Difficult Conversation* (Grand Rapids, MI.: Zondervan, 2015), 24.

5. Joyce Meyer, *Beauty for Ashes: Receiving Emotional Healing* (New York: Warner Faith, 1994), www.goodreads.com/quotes/404426-god-wants-you-to-be -delivered-from-what-you-have.

# More *SUDDENLY SINGLE* resources

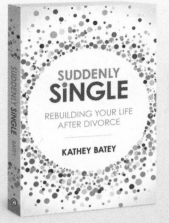

**SUDDENLY SINGLE**
A Compassionate Guide through the Challenges of Divorce

**SUDDENLY SINGLE WORKBOOK**
An Eight-Week Journey into Your New Life Story

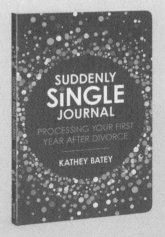

**SUDDENLY SINGLE JOURNAL**
A Place to Process, Plan, and Dream Again

Available wherever books are sold

## DAVID C COOK

*transforming lives together*